American Indian Homes

IGLOOS

by Jack Manning

CAPSTONE PRESS
a capstone imprint

First Facts are published by Capstone Press,
1710 Roe Crest Drive, North Mankato, Minnesota 56003
www.capstonepub.com

Library of Congress Cataloging-in-Publication Data
Manning, Jack.
  Igloos / by Jack Manning.
      pages cm. — (First facts. American Indian homes)
  Includes bibliographical references and index.
    ISBN 978-1-4914-0314-3 (library binding)
    ISBN 978-1-4914-0318-1 (paperback)
    ISBN 978-1-4914-0322-8 (eBook PDF)
1. Igloos—Juvenile literature. 2. Inuit—Dwellings—Juvenile literature. I. Title.
E99.E7M255 2015
693'.91—dc23   2014005135

Editorial Credits
Brenda Haugen, editor; Kyle Grenz, designer; Jo Miller, media researcher;
Kathy McColley, production specialist

Photo Credits
Alamy: North Wind Picture Archives, 19; Cartesia, 6 (map); Corbis: Bettmann, 7; Fotolia:
Malena und Philipp K, 1; Nature Picture Library: Doug Allan, 5; Newscom: ZUMA Press/Ton
Koene, 9, 11, 15; Science Source: Bryan and Cherry Alexander, 17, 21, George Holton, 13;
Shutterstock: Michel Cecconi, cover, Tyler Olson, 3

Design Elements
Shutterstock: paperbees, Tyler Olson

Printed in the United States   5798

Table of Contents

Chapter 1

What Is an Igloo?

Igloos are dome-shaped houses. Some American Indians built igloos made of snow. An igloo sometimes had room for just one person. Others were big enough for families.

Many igloos had porches that looked like tunnels. People crawled through the porches to get inside the igloos.

FACT

Igloos can also be made of sod or wood.

sod—the top layer of soil and the grass attached to it

Who Lived in Igloos?

The Inuit lived in igloos. They are **native** people from the Arctic Circle area. The Inuit live in Greenland, northern Russia, northern Canada, and central Alaska.

The Inuit used igloos on hunting trips. People in the coldest areas of the Arctic lived in igloos all winter.

Where Inuit Live »

① Arctic Circle
② Alaska
③ Russia
④ Canada
⑤ Greenland

native—people who were born in a particular country or place

FACT

Few Inuit live in igloos today. They sometimes build igloos on hunting trips.

Working with Snow

The Inuit made igloos from hard snow. They used knives to cut the snow into blocks. The knives were made of bone, metal, or ivory.

There are many kinds of snow. The Inuit tried to use snow from the same snowfall. That way it would be the same kind. Using different kinds of snow could cause cracks in an igloo.

---

ivory—the natural substance of which the tusks and teeth of some animals are made

Chapter 4

Small or Big?

An Inuit hunter often built a small igloo by himself while out on a hunt. He drew a circle in the snow to mark the igloo's size. The circle was just big enough to lie down in.

People worked together to build larger snow igloos. Family igloos were 6 to 15 feet (2 to 5 meters) wide.

A man marks space for an igloo.

Chapter 5

Building an Igloo

The builder put blocks of snow end to end along the circle. Then the builder stacked blocks in a dome shape.

The last block placed was the keystone. It held all the other pieces together. The builder cut a small hole in the top of the dome for a chimney.

FACT

Builders used blubber oil lamps to melt thin layers of snow inside the igloos. The thin layer froze into ice and helped keep out the wind.

Builders fit blocks of snow together.

keystone—a wedge-shaped piece at the top of an igloo that locks the other blocks of snow in place

blubber—fat under the skin of a whale or a seal

Chapter 6

Inside an Igloo

Inside igloos Inuit families spent time together. They cooked meals and sewed. They also told stories and sang.

Family igloos often had two or three platforms. One platform was covered with willow mats topped by furs or moss. The Inuit slept on these mats.

platform—a flat, raised structure where people can stand or sleep

A family cooks in an igloo.

14

Chapter 7

Igloo Villages

In some parts of Canada, the Inuit built igloo villages. They lived in the igloos during the winter months. Up to 300 people lived in one village.

Families and friends sometimes built tunnels joining igloos together. People could crawl through the tunnels and visit one another. They did not need to walk outside in the cold and wind.

A man finishes an igloo in a small village.

Chapter 8

Special Igloos

Special igloos were sometimes built for ceremonies and dances. In Thule, Greenland, the Inuit built large igloos called snow domes. People in the village often gathered there during long winter nights. They held singing, dancing, and wrestling events in these igloos.

ceremony—formal actions, words, and often music performed to mark an important occasion

Inuit people told stories in special igloos.

Letting in Light

Igloos let in plenty of light. During the day the sun shone through the layer of ice and lit the home. At night blubber oil lamps provided light and heat.

In winter some people still build snow igloos for warmth. During long trips across Canada, people use snow igloos for shelter.

Amazing but True

How can a house made of snow and ice stay warm? The Inuits found ways to stay comfortable in their igloos. A blubber oil lamp could warm an igloo to 90 degrees Fahrenheit (32 degrees Celsius).

Glossary

blubber (BLUH-bur)—fat under the skin of a whale or a seal

ceremony (SER-uh-moh-nee)—formal actions, words, and often music performed to mark an important occasion

ivory (EYE-vur-ee)—the natural substance of which the tusks and teeth of some animals are made

keystone (KEE-stohn)—a wedge-shaped piece at the top of an igloo that locks the other blocks of snow in place

native (NAY-tiv)—people who were born in a particular country or place

platform (PLAT-form)—a flat, raised structure where people can stand or sleep

sod (SOD)—the top layer of soil and the grass attached to it

Read More

Lynch, Wayne. *Arctic A to Z.* Richmond Hill, Ont.: Firefly Books, 2009.

Schuh, Mari C. *Look Inside an Igloo.* Look Inside. Mankato, Minn.: Capstone Press, 2009.

Spilsbury, Louise A. *Igloos and Inuit Life.* The Big Picture. Mankato, Minn.: Capstone Press, 2011.

Internet Sites

FactHound offers a safe, fun way to find Internet sites related to this book. All of the sites on FactHound have been researched by our staff.

Here's all you do:

Visit *www.facthound.com*

Type in this code: 9781491403143

Check out projects, games and lots more at
www.capstonekids.com

Index

Critical Thinking Using the Common Core

1. Is a certain kind of snow used to make igloos? Does it matter what kind of snow is used? Say why. (Key Ideas and Details)

2. Look at the Fact box on page 9. What is the author trying to say? Do you think it would be easier to use a saw or a knife to build an igloo? Say why. (Integration of Knowledge and Ideas)